99

Northern Shaolin Style

Shaolin #1
Open the Door

開
門

Rick L. Wing

Jing Mo Association
San Francisco, California

Published by

Jing Mo Association

San Francisco, California

www.jingmo.com

ISBN   0-9771648-1-0

Disclaimer

Please note that the author and publisher of this book are not responsible in any manner whatsoever for any injury that may result from practicing the techniques and/or following the instructions given in this book. Since the physical activities described may be too strenuous in nature to engage in safely, it is essential that a physician be consulted prior to training.

先慈　歐愛好女士

謹以此書獻給

This book is dedicated to
Anita Ow Wing
(1931 – 2005)

Preface

I was not sure how far I'd get in this "series." Honestly, I did not envision doing anything past the "Martial Skill" book on Shaolin #5. I thought that was it. First and last one, done! However, a few people nudged me a bit, so I thought I'd give it a try with another. I wasn't sure if I would ever get to all the rest so I thought I should try Shaolin #1, which is a top set of our style (how about "subculture?"). I figured that if I could do Shaolin #1 in book form, the others would also be possible. And if I ever do the rest, I honestly don't even know in what order the books will come out - but they will come out! I earnestly hope that people will understand that the purpose of these books is to spread friendship and a sense of community among martial arts practitioners, especially those of the Northern Shaolin Style. Some high-level practitioners have told me that this is an important endeavor. Hopefully, practitioners of the Northern Shaolin Style will enjoy this book as much as I've enjoyed this set.

I myself learned the form "Shaolin #1" from my teacher, Grandmaster Wong Jack Man. He called it "Siu Lum 1" and since he called it that, so did I. He never used Mandarin at all, only Cantonese. Looking back, I feel it was quite an honor to learn this style from someone I consider a true master of the Northern Shaolin Style. He was the great master who taught me this style when I was young. I have also heard it said that "Change is the only constant." Well, I suppose that I am not young anymore, so … change happens. When I became older I was sometimes called upon to teach and demonstrate the more difficult moves of this set, but I did so only at the request of my teacher.

However, in the opinion of my fellow students and others around the world, our teacher, Wong Jack Man Sifu, will always be the great master. I believe there is another expression that goes "Some things never change."

After teaching Chinese martial arts consistently and faithfully for 45 years, Master Wong retired on December 28, 2005, and has left a tremendous legacy in the martial world. I wish him the very best, and I thank him for allowing me to follow in his path.

With respect,

Rick L. Wing
October 2, 2010
San Francisco, California

Author's Foreword

This book details an advanced form of the Northern Shaolin Style, namely Shaolin #1, which is also known as "Open the Door." It is difficult to show the dynamic nature of this form using photographs, but at the very least, we hope we have given the flavor of the set. This book may be used as an aid in learning the form, or for those who already know the form, simply as a reference. Trust your own teacher to guide you. For those who already know the form, do not allow this book to supersede your own instructor's teachings. It should also be expected that the various lineages will have slight differences in their methods. Perhaps you may even use this book as a basis with which to begin discussion of the form and its applications. Please relax, take some time, and enjoy this book at your leisure.

Calligraphy and Inscription of Grandmaster Chan Kwok Wai

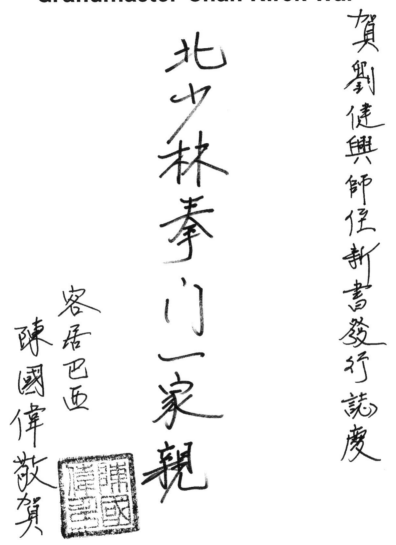

Congratulations to my martial nephew, Rick L. Wing
(Low Gin Hing / Liu Jian Xing), on publishing his new book.

The Northern Shaolin Style is One United Family!

Respectfully submitted by Chan Kwok Wai (Chen Guo Wei)
from Sao Paulo, Brazil.

Grandmaster Chan Kwok Wai

Chan Kwok Wai was born in 1936, in Taishan, Guangdong Province, in southern China. His interest in the martial arts flourished at an early age. At the age of four, he was caught spying on Master Chan Chuk Hsing, the local village master, while attempting to imitate the Choy Li Fut movements he saw. Those who caught the youngster took him immediately to the master in order to see him punished for surreptitiously observing the practice session, but instead, after asking to see what the young Chan had learned while spying, the master was so impressed by little Chan's natural ability that he invited him to be a regular student! Thus, the young Chan Kwok Wai studied under Chan Chuk Hsing for the next ten years learning the art of Choy Li Fut.

A while later and by chance, Chan Kwok Wai learned that his next-door neighbor, a very quiet and humble old man, was in fact Yim Seung Mo (Yan Shangwu), a Cantonese kung fu master who had been a Hung Gar teacher for many years. In his early thirties, Yim, after having been defeated in a friendly match by the highly acclaimed Northern Shaolin master Gu Ruzhang, gave up his Hung Gar and decided to follow Master Gu. Yim eventually became one of Gu's top students.

Yim accepted Chan Kwok Wai as his student after Chan demonstrated his deep desire to learn. Yim started teaching Chan Kwok Wai and a small group on the roof top of an apartment building. Besides teaching the Northern Shaolin Style which he had learned from Gu Ruzhang, Yim also taught styles he had learned from other masters such as the Natural Style and the Six Harmonies Style from Wan Lai Sing. Yim also learned the arts of Xing Yi, Bagua Zhang, and Choy Li Fut.

Later, one of Yim's students helped him to establish his own school in Hong Kong. At this school in Hong Kong, many had the good fortune to learn from this gifted and honorable man.

In 1960 Chan Kwok Wai emigrated to São Paulo, Brazil. It was there that he established his school and became one of the first to teach the authentic art of kung fu to the people of Brazil. Chan Kwok Wai's many students have helped spread Yim's legacy throughout Brazil and abroad. On April 11, 2010, Chan Kwok Wai students celebrated the 50th anniversary of Grandmaster Chan's arrival in Brazil. May Grandmaster Chan continue to spread his knowledge for many years to come!

Submitted by Roberto "Beto" Baptista

The official photograph of Master Chan Kwok Wai celebrating his fiftieth anniversary of teaching martial art in Brazil.

Yim Seung Mo (seated center) at a gathering of his students in Hong Kong. Chan Kwok Wai stands (with tie) at the right shoulder of Yim Seung Mo.

Foreword on Shaolin #1, Open the Door

By Sifu Kisu

July 1, 2010

What does one say when the head of a legendary branch of traditional Chinese martial arts asks you to write a preface for his book detailing one of the most, if not the most, difficult training sets in the Northern Shaolin System?

I was humbled by his request, and would first like to tell you how we met. I was first introduced to Rick by his classmate, Daniel Carr. This occurred prior to the time that Grandmaster Wong Jack Man retired from public teaching and turned his San Francisco school over to Rick. For many years, Rick has been a disciple of Grandmaster Wong Jack Man, a legend of the Northern Shaolin Style. Since then we have met and have become excellent friends. I respect Rick for his humility, his dedication to the art, and for his high level of skill which can clearly be seen by the photos in this book. Rick gives his time freely and he adheres to the highest standards in the transmission of the art to all willing and respectful students. We have talked about the art, and have also shared many a laugh together. The time spent was enjoyable, and we shall see each other again. Our only real competition seems to be who has the best jokes, and although I think we're about tied, I am guessing he thinks he has the edge.

Now, I would like to tell you a bit about myself. My name is Kisu, and for the past 30 years I have been a daily practitioner of the Northern Shaolin Style, a complete system of traditional martial cultivation. Because of this practice, I have experienced great benefit and blessing as the practice of Northern Shaolin has transformed me completely, in mind, body, and spirit, to become not only confident and strong, but also calm and patient.

I would like to offer one of my favorite quotes from a book by Terence Duke:

"Chuan Fa (Fist Arts) embodied harmonized teaching and training which could serve as either self-defense, healing, psychological revelation, vivifying exercise, or a spiritual path, and could act as a catalyst to people who would normally not be interested in spiritual principles or other training."[1]

The above is one of my favorite quotations about the essence and nature of kung fu training. It is also a powerful description of my own personal experience relating to Northern Shaolin.

Originally, I approached martial art in an effort to control the physical world around me and to learn how to defend myself. Instead, I slowly realized that the key toward self-control would be the infusion of my "spiritual" self into every aspect of my "physical" self by using the practice and doctrines of the Northern Shaolin method and its related connections to

[1] "The Bodhisattva Warriors," by Terence Duke, 1994, Weiser Books. Pg. 226.

Chinese philosophy and culture.

I now realize that my own teacher, Sifu Hui Ho Kwong (Ken Hui) had to bridge a vast cultural gulf between him and me. I thank him for this because if he did not do this, it would have been very difficult for me to even begin to understand the lessons he had in store for me. I salute his patience and am extremely grateful for his lessons. I know now that I was less than an ideal candidate. He has improved me immeasurably.

Sifu Hui is a sincere teacher and is willing to teach anyone that comes to learn from him. He will tell you everything he knows about the art, provided that you are a sincere and honest student. At the same time though, he is also a demanding teacher. He wants each of his students to be excellent in practice but does not require that they be a champion in competition or performance. Competition is decidedly of secondary importance to him. Character is primary. He patiently taught us the discipline of traditional Chinese martial art and he fully expects that all of his students abide by the traditional relationship between martial art master and student.

This is a very foreign concept to most westerners due to our overly competitive nature. We are taught to value ourselves highly, but this may also prove to be an impediment towards true learning, as it is sometimes difficult for us to humble ourselves enough to learn the wisdom of others. In seems that in modern day society, we are taught to value ourselves at the expense of others. I have found that an inflated sense of self is not very useful. Reverence toward a teacher is rare and sometimes we may even be defiant or resentful of this relationship. However, I fully believe that these teachings deserve deep reverence, as over time they will enrich and uplift one's life for the better. How can one truly respect the teachings if one does not respect the master?

The word "sifu" may be literally translated as "teacher-father" in English. My own teacher, Sifu Hui carefully explained to me the sacrifices he himself had to make in order to learn the martial arts. He then explained that his teacher taught him in the same tradition. The first time I visited Sifu Hui's school, I saw his kung fu and was impressed beyond words. By his movements I could see that he knew the essence of traditional Northern Shaolin Style. Although he accepted me as a student, I believe it took a long time for him to actually trust me. After many years his teachings finally took root in me. I now stand as a dedicated disciple of his teachings, a daily practitioner, and also a teacher of the Northern Shaolin Style.

Sifu Hui is very talented, especially in terms of remembering and perceiving the true meaning of the techniques in the forms. He himself trained very hard, and because of this, he knows how to apply the techniques in the forms. He taught me that the pursuit is never-ending for one wishing to follow the true martial way. Martial art is a way of life. It is a path towards the development of personal happiness. The forms and complete curriculum of the Northern Shaolin Style are designed to lead the practitioner through the various stages of development.

My teacher himself learned from a talented and dedicated man named So Bin Yuen (Johnny So), who in turn learned from an amazing teacher named Yim Seung Mo. Yim Seung Mo was a true disciple of the great master Gu Ruzhang. Gu Ruzhang was an acclaimed master of the iron palm and iron body, and was well known throughout the whole of China. Sifu Wong Jack Man was also a student of Master Yim Seung Mo. In this little known discipline of Northern Shaolin, Rick and I are similar to brothers in a family that transcends nationality, borders, race, and religion, and this brings us closer as human beings. If not for this rare treasure, would we even be known to one another as brothers and lifelong friends? In all probability, I believe we would not, but as it has turned out, this is the case.

Let me now discuss the Northern Shaolin Style. The Northern Shaolin Style is one of the most prominent of the traditional northern methods. The northern styles of kung fu generally emphasize long range techniques, quick advances and retreats, wide low stances, kicking and leaping techniques, whirling circular blocks, aggressive attacks, and the qualities of speed and agility. Gu Ruzhang's Northern Shaolin Style consists of ten forms, and each form is intended to be a comprehensive lesson on a specific aspect of kung fu. These are not to be mistaken as ten artistic routines. Each of these forms has a theme, and it is up to us, as modern day practitioners, to discover and ponder these themes. An accomplished student of this style should pursue and develop insight into the deep meaning of each form through constant practice. He should carefully analyze the techniques and combinations shown in the style.

The essence and teachings of the ancient masters are expressed in these forms. The Northern Shaolin Style has proven to be an effective and broad-based pool of knowledge. The sets have deep meaning if deep thought is given to them. Not all practitioners of the style will gain the same insight from these forms due to their own differences in background, training, and point of view. Most importantly, it is the pursuit of this understanding that should be our primary goal.

The set exhibited in this book, namely Shaolin #1, is made up of combinations of physically demanding techniques. The purpose of this set is not only to teach the student useful hand techniques, kicking techniques, aerial techniques, and ground techniques, but also to develop the physical attributes of flexibility and balance, along with a high level of leaping and acrobatic ability. At the same time, many of the combinations in the form are actual time-tested applications.

The training of the Northern Shaolin Style follows the process of natural body development. I feel that the Northern Shaolin Style is one of the best systems for training young people. I hope to raise the bar for them and make them better people through my own efforts. The martial methods of Northern Shaolin should help a child's self-confidence and will hopefully channel the child's energies into constructive and useful action. The

Northern Shaolin martial methods mean much more and are more than a vehicle for mere fighting. They are a vehicle for the cultivation of self-control, as well as self-defense. When a child learns self-control and self-discipline, what goal can possibly remain out of reach? The art of mastering the Northern Shaolin Style is a difficult path, but one that is extremely rewarding. In the physical realm, a child learns to control the body through the forms and the techniques. By controlling the body, a child learns to discipline the mind and to strengthen the connection of the mind with the body. To be able to push the body beyond endurance, through determination and sheer willpower, is something that is of great value. In this wonderful union of mind and body, the rewards are potentially without limit. Through the growth experience of Northern Shaolin training, a child learns more than just how to defend himself. He or she also learns the initial steps towards becoming a more positive, constructive, and contributing member of our society.

The Northern Shaolin Style has proven to be an effective and broad-based pool of martial knowledge. It deserves our strongest efforts and we must allow the Northern Shaolin Style to benefit others in the future.

I personally vow to continue my pursuit of excellence in the martial arts as a way of life, and I hope to help others reach new heights in their development and their martial endeavors.

Peace.
Sifu Kisu
Southern California, USA

Lineage Chart:

This chart shows how the collaborators as referenced in the early part of the book are related in the martial world.

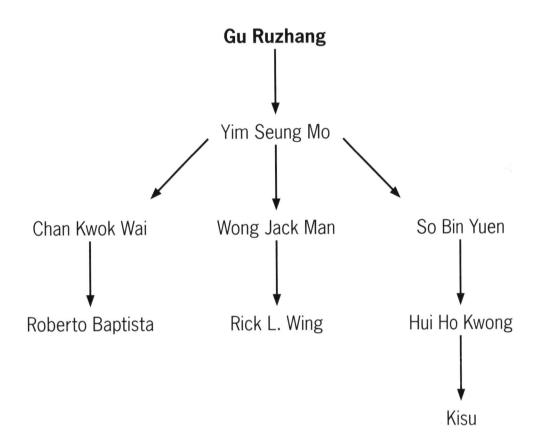

Table of Contents

Commentary on Shaolin #1

Commentary on Shaolin #1

The Northern Shaolin System is one of the few systems from the Shaolin Temple that has been passed down relatively intact and complete. There are ten sets in this style, and some consider this set to be the premier set of the style. This is one of the longer and more advanced forms and is a set densely packed with kicking techniques, sweeps, and ground maneuvers. This beautiful and dynamic set "opens the door" to the famed Northern Shaolin Style. In the previous book, "Shaolin #5, Martial Skill," the history of Northern Shaolin Style was discussed and the flavor of each of the ten forms was shown with a few selected moves. The form Shaolin #5, along with Shaolin #6, #7, #8 and #4, is one of the five shorter forms of the style. The long forms are numbered 1, 2, 3, 9, and 10. Another book on the short form, "Shaolin #6, Close Strike," will be geared towards beginning students. This book on Shaolin #1 is for the advanced and experienced practitioners of the style.

This form, called "Open the Door" or "Enter the Gate" is so named because this set "opens the door" to the Northern Shaolin Style. However, this does not necessarily mean that it is the first set taught. Rather, it is most likely called "Open the Door" because it allows the advanced practitioner to practice moves that demonstrate a more complete understanding of the Northern Shaolin Style. It might also be thought that long ago, this set was taught only to certain students of the system, and therefore these students might be said to have attained a higher level of martial ability. Nowadays, anyone can learn these things, but it should be mentioned that real ability still takes hard work (so I've been told), and trust me, I have searched long and hard for the easy way. I have finally come to the conclusion that serious practice is the key to serious ability.

After learning many of the other sets of the Northern Shaolin Style, I must admit that this set put it all together for me. I had a lot of fun learning this set. It was a set that definitely continued the pattern of the other forms, but also raised the system to a higher level. Shaolin #3 was longer, but I thought that Shaolin #1 was more fun to practice, that is, when I had the energy. Shaolin #3 was a set that was easier to do -- if you did it slowly. It was hard to do Shaolin #1 "slowly" because of all the jumps and kicks. The movements of Shaolin #3 were not particularly difficult, and there were as many kicks (36), but it was just that the set Shaolin #3 was very long, and with lower horse stances. Also, the kicks in Shaolin #3 seemed to come off stances that made the kicks feel more awkward in their execution. I suppose it is "practice" that is supposed to make the movements less awkward to perform. The movements of Shaolin #1 seemed to flow more easily and smoothly, especially when executing the many kicks. In comparison to the other Shaolin forms, Shaolin #1 was more dynamic and explosive with respect to the kicking and sweeping techniques. And of course, it goes without saying (but let me say it anyway!) that this is just my opinion, probably molded by my own body type, my own practice and experience, and my own

3

peculiar thought processes. I have spoken with many Northern Shaolin practitioners over the decades and trust me; everyone has a different opinion regarding favorite moves, favorite sets, philosophy, etc. Whatever meaning this set takes on for you, so be it.

Shaolin #1 was a difficult mountain for me to climb, but slowly I got there. This set was not easy to do, as it was a set that required a great deal of drive, energy, and concentration. At least it required that for me personally. I was only satisfied with doing this set if it was done in a way that I thought proper. Those days were few. Jumping through the air, kicking, landing in a split, jumping out of it, rolling around on the ground, jumping up again … this was something that I really had to gear up for. Maybe there are some people who might practice this set first, but for me, no way, I was definitely not that good.

What do I think the ancients tried to show us by handing down these special movements? I believe the monks long ago used this form to develop a high level of athleticism in case they needed this type of exceptional physical ability with which to fight. Because there are so many kicks in this form, I believe this form, more so than the others, was developed to build agility and stamina, and to enhance kicking ability. Some practitioners have suggested to me that this is the set whereby a student is taught to defend himself by using a barrage of kicks.

This set has most of the kicks that are in the Northern Shaolin System, not all, but most. The interesting thing about this set is that it is the one set that uses kicks and sweeps at the varying levels: low, medium, and high. There are leg-flower ground rolling techniques, standing kicks, and also jumping kicks. There are a great deal of moves that involve being down on the ground, and then leaping up to do a jump kick. In this set, it is necessary to twist your body to gain the proper momentum to carry you into the next movement. You will understand this if you know the other sets and compare them with Shaolin #1. Many sweeps and kicks are also placed together in sequence with a minimum of intervening hand techniques. Some of the highlighted movements of this set are the butterfly kick (also called "Swallow flies through the curtain"), the left leg tornado kick, the low left leg hooking kick, the split (also in Shaolin #9), the backhand slap followed by the crane's beak strike, and the leg-flower ground rolling technique. There are also two "grind the bowl" sweeps in this set, which is more than any other set has. Most of the other movements or some variation thereof, appear in the other forms.

Movement #46, called "Swallow flies through the curtain" is also known as the butterfly kick. This movement is the best known move in the entire set. It is an aesthetically pleasing movement that is also very common in Peking Opera. This movement should feel good to the practitioner as the practitioner will temporarily "fly" through the air. This particular move may also be considered as an exercise useful in toning the waist. Although it is possible to use this move for combat, keep in mind that it is a move that should be used sparingly. Hopefully, you might be lucky and catch your opponent unawares and retreating. If you can do this, you are in good shape (yes, that was intended). I myself have been kicked in the face with this technique and knocked flat on my back, so I know that it is possible to use this kick in actual combat

Probably the second best known move in the set is movement #49. This move is called "one character leg" and is the name the Chinese use for a split. This is another move that people usually identify with Shaolin #1, although this move is also in Shaolin #9. The split is a move that is designed to increase flexibility and agility. Although some might say that every movement in a set has an application, providing an application for this move would be a bit of a stretch (also intended). I suppose that anyone could imagine and create a scenario where this move could be used in combat, but I would consider that to be rather fanciful and probably more applicable for martial arts movie choreography. It is risky to be down in the split position while someone is intent on causing you severe physical injury, and unless you have the capability of rising back up instantly, I personally would not try something of this nature. Suffice it to say that the move is good exercise.

Another well-known movement in this set would be the leg scissors techniques of movement #58. This movement is aesthetically pleasing and is also useful as exercise for the waist. These movements, if the practitioner knows how to skillfully apply them, are very useful if the practitioner ends up on the ground. I myself have ended up on the ground many times, and most unwillingly. While on the ground the practitioner can still defend himself and attack the legs and balance of the opponent. Applications for this are shown in the applications section of the book.

I believe that Shaolin #1 is also a set which really brings out a practitioner's personal style, more so than in the other forms. As this set may be considered difficult for some people, including myself, let us examine the things that make a set look different from person to person. Although we may all be doing the same set, there is a great deal of variety in the final outcome. This might be equated to comparing people's handwriting, which is so individual that banks and stores sometimes require it for identification purposes. First, let us look at a person's reason for practice. Some may do the set in a manner they believe is more appropriate for applications, as opposed to physical exercise or performance. For example, if he wants to emphasize certain self-defense aspects, he may want to place greater importance on the twisting and grasping motions of the hands prior to the execution of a punch or a kick. Or he may direct his strikes to what he considers the appropriate level, so he might want to keep his kicks at stomach, or perhaps face level, depending on what his target is. If a person wants to do the set for exercise purposes, he may want to extend his movements further so as to increase the capabilities of his body. And for exercise purposes, some will want to go slowly, so as to develop their legs and sit in the horse stances more deeply and for a slightly longer period of time, while others will go more quickly in order to improve their stamina and aerobic capacity. A deeper horse stance allows for more stability, while a higher horse allows for increased mobility. How quickly a person does the set depends on what aspect of training he is trying to improve. If a person is doing a set for performance, he might do the movements in such a way as to enhance the visual aspects of the form, such as making the motions look larger and grander, thereby making the set look pleasing to the audience. If a person wanted to do the set more for the application aspects, he might also keep the "wind-up" motions to a minimum, so as to conceal the actual attack. There is also the possibility that he may want to wind up more so as to get extra power in his strikes. Of course, not all of these considerations need be mutually exclusive. The main idea is to make the set work for you, while you are working the set.

Another variable that goes into the look of a set is the body build of the practitioner. A person may be thin, stocky, frail, strong, short, tall, young, old, short-armed, long-armed, short-legged, long-legged, bow-legged, etc., and this will be a key reason as to why people's forms look different. Also, a practitioner may be a beginner or an advanced practitioner, and because of the varying levels of expertise, the form will look different. Hopefully, with practice and experience, we should all get better.

As an example, let us look at the tornado kick. Some will swing their arms ever so slightly to get the momentum, while others will swing their arms a great deal. Some will swing their left leg in a big circle, so as to get more momentum for the right leg kick. Others will make the left leg move in a tight circle, as they want the right leg kick to come out quicker. Others will go for the height of the kick, while others will emphasize the torque of the kick. A shorter, stockier person may not be able to jump as high, but the kick might be heavier were it to strike someone. All these variables together conspire to make us look unique when doing a form.

As another example, let us look at the jumping lotus kick. Some, to emphasize the practicality of the movement, will take little wind-up with their arms, so as not to give away the attack, and will jump forward and kick at face level. They want the technique to be done quickly and without fanfare. Another practitioner might consider the arm motion as a blocking or clearing motion, and so will block with a large circular motion, and then jump in high and forward, as if to catch a retreating opponent. This person wants to cover distance and use power. The possibilities are many and they are all valid. In general, the more a person winds up, the more telegraphed the move will be; however, it should have more power. The less telegraphed the technique, the faster it will be executed; however, it may not have as much power. There are always trade-offs to consider when doing the movements.

Putting your own stamp on Shaolin #1 is the important thing. Have fun with this advanced set, and enjoy yourself. As long as no one says "What set is THAT?" or "Is that Shaolin #2?" you're probably on the right track. Even I do this set differently now that I am older. I like to tell people that I am doing the movements with more precision, instead of … well, maybe I'm just getting slower... or perhaps I just imagined that I used to go a little more quickly in the ... old days. Practitioners! Ever hear this before?

Like any other martial system, the Northern Shaolin Style has a certain amount of theory that goes along with it; however, to truly understand the style, it is best to experience the movements on a regular basis. Good luck, friend.

Northern Shaolin Kung Fu

by Sifu Michelle Dwyer

Northern Shaolin Kung Fu

by Sifu Michelle Dwyer

The Northern Shaolin Style originated about a thousand years ago in northern China and traces its roots back to the celebrated Shaolin temple. Large, flowing movements with leaps and flying kicks characterize this style. The system develops speed, strength, and endurance, as well as quick reaction and sensitivity. Athletically elegant as well as demanding, the style has practical fighting techniques designed specifically for the cultivation of full body power. The core of the Northern Shaolin Style is the ten numbered forms, and supplementing these are other forms such as Tam Tuei and various weapons and two person sparring forms.

Master Wong Jack Man came to San Francisco in 1963. He began teaching publicly in his school, which he named the San Francisco Jing Mo Athletic Association. He was the first master to come to the United States to teach the Northern Shaolin Style. In the early years, Master Wong Jack Man taught kung fu six days a week, and then, as the years passed, he slowly lightened his teaching load to two or three days a week. He retired from teaching on December 28, 2005 and although his studio continues, we miss him dearly.

He was a totally dedicated teacher, never missing a class and never canceling a class. Because of the strength of his own personal training, he was never ill and he was always there to share his skill and knowledge. He has deep knowledge of many systems and has left the martial arts world a vast legacy. Tall and thin, relaxed in movement, quiet in temperament, Master Wong is humble and private but nonetheless still well known and highly respected in the martial arts world.

Master Wong Jack Man taught in the traditional manner with clarity and purpose. There was seemingly no order to his class. People arrived, did their own warm-up exercises, practiced their forms, learned from the master, and worked at their own pace. There was no hierarchy, no tests, and no rankings. Visitors who came to his class had to ask "Who is the teacher?" "Which one is the teacher?" This showed how quiet and unassuming the teacher was. All the students knew who the teacher was, but the casual observer would not be sure. People trained at their own level. Sifu taught people at their own rate of learning. Always patient, he used body motion instead of verbal direction to instruct. One had to persevere, study hard, and carefully observe the teacher. Always subtle, the knowledge was there for the observant student to study. His thinking seemed to be that students learned best when they were ready to learn. When asked a question, if he didn't have a ready answer, he would come back the next time as he walked around the room, or the next class with an answer or opinion. The discussion could go on for weeks on an interesting topic. Sifu was always generous in sharing his high level skill and deep knowledge.

One of his most subtle lessons was one of the last that I was to learn from him, even after he retired. Always, through the years, I would observe the Sifu slowly circling the studio as people practiced, giving a lesson here, giving a lesson there. As he slowly circumnavigated the room, he would, in a very relaxed manner, punch the air in various combinations over and over again. I must admit that, in my ignorance, I would joke about the teacher's relaxed punches at the air. "Oh! The teacher's the one over there punching the air." I thought nothing of it. As an older practitioner of kung fu, I am continually working to develop speed, strength, power, technique, and accuracy. All good qualities. I found out from a visiting sifu from China that the highest level of practice is repeated, relaxed, accurate execution of technique. Oh! I had observed our sifu doing this for years, and I did not realize what he was showing me. Sifu, thank you for the excellent education you have given me over the years, for the love of training you have inspired in me, for dedicating your life to this art form, for teaching others, and for keeping this ancient knowledge alive. The art surely lives in you!

At his San Francisco Jing Mo Athletic Association, Master Wong taught Yang Style Tai Chi Chuan, Hsing-I, Northern Shaolin kung fu, Lo Han and various weapons and sparring forms. Wong Jack Man's Tai Chi Chuan was distinctive and excellent, relaxed and refined. One can see the quality of the teacher's moves in the moves of his students. At the very least, we tried to make it so. Many good push-hands people came out of his studio.

The Hsing-I that Master Wong shared is clean, precise, powerful, and inspired with the fighting spirit of the five elements and the twelve animals. This style is very practical and deceptively simple. Master Wong moved with relaxed power as he shared this soft/hard style with his students.

The elegant Northern Shaolin forms are beautiful and demanding with large flowing movements, flying kicks, deep stances, and high leaps. When Sifu Wong demonstrated this style, he was smooth and effortless. When performing the flying kicks, he seemed to stay suspended in the air. He remained flexible, strong, fast and fluid throughout the years. I have been exposed to many styles of martial arts at national and international tournaments and events, and Northern Shaolin ranks with the best of these in terms of power, elegance, and athletic challenge. It has been an honor for me to learn this style from the first master to come to the United States to spread the art of Northern Shaolin. I am proud to be one of the few women in the history of Jing Mo, San Francisco to learn all ten numbered forms.

I joined the San Francisco Jing Mo Athletic Association in 1980 and have been practicing Northern Shaolin ever since. The knowledge and skill of Master Wong and some of his long-time students inspired me to train regularly and learn all the sets as well as many of the weapons and sparring forms. The ten sets of Northern Shaolin are a special challenge as they are physically demanding. The body of information is vast, and the forms are long and need to be memorized and internalized. Each set is unique and the many repeating combinations and rhythms demand mental focus as well as maximum physical exertion.

Though Shaolin #1 is the shortest of the advanced long forms, it is filled with flying kicks, sweeps, splits, and floor techniques. Since I did not think I would be able to do this set very well, like many other students, I saved Shaolin #1 for last. I must admit that every time I do this set, I consider it a challenge for me. After practicing this set for many years, I still consider it to be a challenge! The set is very lively, has more than thirty kicks, and there is no place to catch one's breath! To see Shaolin #1 performed with skill and gusto is a treat indeed!

This brings me to write about the new sifu of the San Francisco Jing Mo Athletic Association. As I mentioned earlier, Sifu Wong retired from teaching on December 28, 2005, after having dedicated himself to teaching for more than forty years. He passed his legacy of martial arts to his many students. His own school, San Francisco Jing Mo Athletic Association, was entrusted to a very dedicated and talented student who we all called "Bucky." Everyone, including the teacher, called him that so I shall use that name too. The studio remains in very capable hands. Bucky is friendly and funny with a wide range of talents. He himself has taught martial art for more than 25 years, and has done many demonstrations and lion dance at many cultural and community gatherings. I could not put a number on how many times he has demonstrated. He demonstrated in the San Francisco Chinese New Year Parade many times. He was very dedicated to training and never missed a class of Sifu Wong's if he could help it. He also trained like his clothes were on fire every time he came to class! At least that is what I saw with my own eyes. You know how people who do things well make them look so easy? Bucky moves quickly and with an energy and flexibility that reminds one of the martial practitioners of old. Perhaps I am even understating this. He makes doing the Shaolin forms look easy. Everybody wants to do it, but he really does it, and in his own unique manner I might add. I admire the spirit and quality of his movement, and also his knowledge of martial application. He also has the ability to inspire and organize people. We have done lion dance together for many years in San Francisco. Our team would meet at the home of his mother, Anita Wing, a person whose life was dedicated to teaching. She was always happy to have her house filled with kung fu people, complete with many children running about. These cultural events were always fun, exciting and entertaining, not only because of Bucky's unique outlook and humorous comments, which came rapidly and continually for those who really knew him, but also because of the connection to the community, of the respect built between cultures, and the respect between generations.

Training the Northern Shaolin Style keeps one healthy and increases the vital energy. I believe it is important to keep this traditional art alive by learning it, training it, teaching it, and sharing it. Every day I thank all my teachers. I have been teaching since 1982 and I find a special delight in sharing Northern Shaolin. People enjoy the rhythm of the style, along with all the flying kicks and the flowing, long movements. My students have ranged in age from twelve to ninety-four, and I have taught people from Oakland to Amsterdam. It is especially rewarding to see grandmothers bloom with vigorous energy when doing the sparring forms. I thank my students for helping me to learn how to teach and explore these art forms on a different level. I consider training to be self-therapeutic on many levels: physical, mental, emotional and spiritual. The best fighting is within myself, as I strive to better myself with each practice or teaching session. Though the knowledge is ancient, the search for self-cultivation is still timeless and never-ending.

A Brief History of Master Gu Ruzhang

by Tan Fengya

Gu Ruzhang

A Brief History of Master Gu Ruzhang of the Northern Shaolin Style
by Tan Fengya

Our Chinese martial arts have a long and illustrious history. It is a combination of sport and art which originated from our folk tradition and has been in development for thousands of years. The methods of Shaolin kung fu are considered by many to be the best in the world.

Shaolin kung fu originated from the Shaolin Temple on Song Mountain of Henan Province. Its formation and development is due to the efforts of many monks in the temple. The monks combined a folk tradition of bodybuilding and fighting skills to create hand forms, weapon forms, and sparring sets. Shaolin kung fu is rich in content and it constitutes a complete and entire system. Shaolin kung fu developed into two distinct schools—the school of northern Shaolin and the school of southern Shaolin.

Master Gu Ruzhang is the great teacher who introduced the martial arts of the Northern Shaolin Style to southern China.

He learned Northern Shaolin Boxing, Large Golden Bell Shield, Small Golden Bell Shield, and Iron Sand Palm from Yan Jiwen (member of the school of the Shaolin Temple on Song Mountain) from Shandong Province; Taiji and Taiji Sword from General Li Jinglin, the chief of the Guangling Seven Swordsmen; Zha Style Boxing from Yu Zhensheng, the famous master of Zha Style; and Xingyi Quan and Taiji from Sun Lutang, the great master of Sun Style Taiji. Master Gu practiced very hard in the twelve years that he spent with Yan Jiwen. Master Gu also wrote a book on the method of Taiji Boxing.

In 1922, he was employed as the captain of the guard by Yan Jiachi—the General-Director of the Finance Department of Guangdong Province. In 1926, he was employed as an instructor at the Central Martial Arts Academy (Zhang Zhijiang being the director and Li Jinglin the deputy director). In 1928, Master Gu won the highest level award in the

National Kung Fu Examination and in the same year, he was employed as a chief instructor of the Guangdong and Guangxi Martial Arts Center (established by Li Jichen, the Military and Political Head of Guangdong Province, and Wan Laisheng, the Director). In 1929, he established the Guangzhou Martial Arts Association located on Wende East Road, close to the Tan San Martial Association which was established by Master Tan San—the famous master of the Choy Lay Fut style. As time passed, these two masters became very good friends and they exchanged students so that their students could be exposed to different arts. At that time, the disciples of Master Gu included: Yan Shangwu, Long Zixiang, Liu Jindong, Chen Zhenbang, Hu Songya (Hu Shaobao), Chen Nianbo, Zheng Xi (Zheng Baili), Chen Xianmin, Xie Chongsheng, Feng De'an, Hu Xianglin and many others.

In 1952, Master Gu died in mainland China for reasons unknown to us, his students. We felt very bad that Master Gu passed away. Instructor Long Zixiang, who was one of Master Gu's chief disciples, reminded us that Master Gu emphasized perseverance, morality, and respect for our ancestors and respect for our martial roots. Master Gu's view was that people in the martial arts should continue to practice industriously, cultivate their character, and cherish the precious cultural heritage that has been handed down by our ancestors. We have the responsibility of handing it down from generation to generation.

The younger generation should keep in mind the many teachings of Master Gu. Uncle Bao, who followed Master Gu for many years, devoted much time and energy to organize this General Commemoration of Master Gu Ruzhang of the Northern Shaolin Style. After working very hard and speaking to many people, he finally obtained the approval of the Societies Registrar Department of the Hong Kong government to establish this group as a legal association. The registrants included Hu Hanxin, Zheng Xi, Long Qiming, Yu Pingzhang, Liang Yiyu, Tan Fengya, and Huang Jinliu, and many others.

As early as 1965, master uncle Yan Shangwu and Long Qiming (son of Long Zixiang) had the thought of establishing the General Commemoration in order to honor and celebrate the birthday of Master Gu Ruzhang. In the years to follow, Master Yan passed away and Long Qiming was committed to doing work for the national service, and so the establishment of the Commemoration was put off time and again. Only now have we finally and formally established our association. This proves the old saying, "When there is a will, there is a way."

Although having little talent and even less learning, I was trusted by many and given an important task. In order to live up to their expectations, I know that I must keep the teachings of our master in mind. We must respect our ancestors and remember our roots. We must promote the Northern Shaolin Style of martial arts widely, both in Hong Kong and all around the world. We must unite and maintain the friendship among all members of all of our schools.

Although I am not capable of learning the entire field of martial arts, I would like to follow the wise men of old and boldly push this large ship of "kung fu" forward. To all concerned, please accept my humble efforts.

Gu Ruzhang in "Single Whip" posture.

Gu Ruzhang in "Golden Rooster Stands on One Leg" posture.

Editor's Note: This was translated from material from the 1st Inaugural Ceremonial Proceedings of the Gu Ruzhang Memorial Association, September 11, 1983, Northern Shaolin Association of Hong Kong. The information was graciously provided by Sifu Paul Fung Ngar Tam of the Northern Shaolin Gu Ruzhang Memorial Association. Sifu Paul F. N. Tam is the former Chairman of the Northern Shaolin Gu Ruzhang Memorial Association in the United States of America.

Shaolin #1: Open the Door - The Form

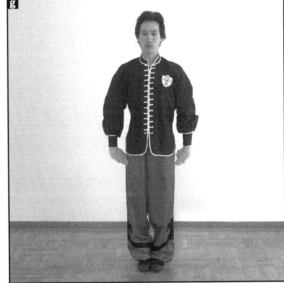

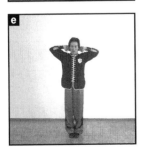

Opening position

Opening Salute: Stand at attention and look straight ahead. Your fists are at your sides. Raise both arms forward and all the way up, and then press down with both palms. This is done in one continuous motion.

一，滾手舞花坐虎勢

1 - Revolving hands dancing with the flowers. Sitting tiger posture.

Turn to your right. Simultaneously, stamp your right foot on the ground and bring your arms together, right over left, with the right palm facing down and the left palm facing up. Using a clockwise motion, turn both hands in a complete circle. The right hand will push out in a palm strike, and the left hand will hook backwards. The left foot will step out as you sit in a left cat stance. (When the hands are moving with a particular circling motion, many times the Chinese characters will utilize the words "dancing with the flowers." The left cat stance is the "Sitting tiger posture.")

二、鳳凰旋窩

2 - Phoenix circling the nest.

Starting with the left foot, take five consecutive steps in a semi-circular path. Left foot, right foot, left foot, right foot, left foot, with the last step being the placing of the left foot alongside the right foot. (The Chinese characters indicate that the phoenix is circling quickly outside of its nest.)

三，仙人拱手

3- Immortal man pays respect with a salute.

While straightening the legs to stand straight up, brush the backs of both hands against the thighs and then push the right fist into the left palm. (The Chinese characters indicate that an immortal is paying respect in a very polite manner with his salute.)

side view

四．舞花单鉤手

4 - Hands dancing with the flowers. Single hooking hand (right).

Bring the right hand over the left hand and form the fingers of the right hand into a hook. Move both hands in a figure '8' motion with the left hand following the right. The left hand moves as an open palm to the "guard" position. The final motion is the swinging of the right arm from behind into an upright position with the right hand becoming a crane's beak.

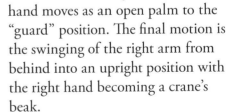

五、坐马听风

5 - Sitting horse listens to the wind.

Step forward with the right leg and stamp the right foot on the ground. When the right foot stamps the ground, the right arm moves over the left arm, right palm facing down and the left palm facing up. After revolving both hands in a complete clockwise circle, the left hand will go forward into a palm strike and the right hand will pull back into a fist. The left foot will move behind the right foot and past it as you sit into a horse stance.

back view

六. 護 心 肘

6 - Covering the heart, elbow strike. (Elbow strike to the heart).

While turning your waist to the left, push the fist of the right hand into the palm of the left hand and extend the right elbow forward. The legs move into a left bow stance. (The Chinese characters for this move do not indicate whether the movement is named for the fact that both of your hands will cover your own heart when you use this elbow strike, or whether the elbow strike is to the opponent's heart.)

七、挑鉤掛打披馬勢

7 - Pulling hook (hand), hanging strike (leg), pressing horse posture.

Both your hands will move in a counterclockwise clearing motion. As the right hand makes a hooking motion from the front to the back, the left palm will push out, and the right leg will hook forward as the body pivots on the left foot.

八、坐马听风

8 - Sitting horse listens to the wind. (Sit in horse, right palm strike).

As the right foot steps down, the right arm slides over the left arm into a right palm strike as the left hand pulls back into a fist.

九、偷步連環通臂掌

9 - Steal a step. Connected links (palms). Penetrating arm (left palm).

As the right foot steps behind the left leg into a left T-stance, the right palm moves down to the midsection while the left palm pushes out. Look in the direction of your left palm. (When the Chinese characters say, "Steal a step," they typically mean that one foot steps behind the other.)

十. 右撑掌左蹬腿

10 - Right crashing palm. Left heel kick.

Turn your head and look over your left shoulder. While the right palm pushes out, throw a left side kick.

十一、掛面腿

11 - Swinging kick to the face.

Bring the left leg down and swing it with a counter-clockwise motion. Push off with the right leg and slap the side of the right foot with the palm of the left hand. (Some would call this kick a leaping, inside crescent kick. When martial artists use the word 'crescent kick, the implication is that the kick is one which travels from the outside to the inside, or comes inward.)

十二. 拍地飛沙

12 - Slap the ground. Flying sand (Throw the sand).

Drop into a right scattered stance and slap both of your hands on the ground. (The implication of the name of this move is that when the ground is slapped, you have the option of picking up sand so that you may throw it into the face of your opponent.

back view

Whether someone wishes to mimic this motion in the set is at the discretion of the practitioner. Another possible interpretation of the words is that the practitioner might slap the ground so hard as to create "flying sand," meaning that the ground was hit so hard that the dust was raised.)

十三, 磨盤腿

13 - Grinding, coiling leg (Grinding the bowl).

Rest your entire weight on both of your hands, and swing the right leg in a counter-clockwise motion so that the right leg passes in front of the left leg and then under the left leg as the left foot is raised up momentarily so that the right leg may revolve in a complete circle. You will end up in the same position as when you first started this move. (The Chinese characters indicate that a millstone is grinding wheat in a circular fashion, and it is this action that is being mimicked with this particular leg technique.)

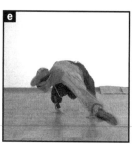

十四、撲腿小關門

14 - Reclining stance. Small closing of the gate.

Rise up into a back leaning horse stance, with 60% of the weight on the left leg, and 40% of the weight on the right leg. The left and right hands will make a grasping clockwise motion in the air with the right hand making a larger circle than the left hand. When both hands come down, they will close into fists. (The Chinese characters for the words "Small closing the gate," indicate that this is a tight circular blocking motion, and are words that are clear to experienced martial artists, but perhaps not to the general public.)

back view

十五．黑虎闯山

15 - Black tiger crashes through the mountain.

Stamp the right foot and block upward with the right arm. Step forward into a left horse stance and strike with the left fist. (The name of the movement should indicate the ferocity with which the movement should be done.)

十六. 鷂子翻身

16A - Sparrow hawk turns its body.

Turn your body to the right and bring the right foot forward by placing it behind the left leg. You will step into a right bow stance. While turning the body, the right hand will first drop down, and then the right hand will rise up and then move in a downward arc.

Strike with the back of the right hand. The left hand moves to the guard position with the palm facing down.

back view

41

十六 ， 掛打鈎竿勢

16B - Hooking pole posture.

Withdraw the right hand slightly in a counter-clockwise motion, and then raise it up to strike with the back of the wrist. The right hand will become a crane's beak as you sit into a horse stance. The left hand remains in the guard position.

back view

十七、掏鈎掛打披馬艷

17 - Pulling hook, hanging strike, pressing horse posture.

Simultaneously, hook the left hand backwards, bring the right hand to the guard position, and sweep forward with the left leg.

十八．左蹬足

18 - Left heel kick.

Letting the left leg continue in its clockwise path, withdraw the left leg to the front of the right leg, and then kick out with the left leg, using the outer edge of the left foot as the striking surface.

back view

十九．泰山压顶

19 - Mount Tai crashes down!

While stepping down into a left bow stance, make a counter-clockwise clearing motion with the left hand and strike the back of the right fist into the palm of the left hand. (The force of your backfist strike is supposed to mimic the awesome destruction that would occur should the great Mount Tai suddenly collapse and destroy all beneath it.)

二十．回身鉤手左蹬足

20 - Turn the body, hooking hands, left heel kick.

While turning your legs into a left T-stance, hook down with the left hand and the right hand, quickly in succession. Throw a left leg side kick.

二十一. 挑鈎掛打披马勢

21 - Pulling hook, hanging strike, pressing horse posture.

Step down with the left leg and bring the right arm forward with the right hand in the crane's beak position. Simultaneously, hook the right hand backwards, push the left palm out, and sweep forward with the right leg.

二十二、烏龍擺尾倒退步

22 - Spinning wheel hands Continuous retreating steps.

Step down with the right foot and make a large counter-clockwise circular motion with the right arm with the fingers of the right hand in the "sword" position. Step behind with the left leg and make a large clockwise circular motion with the left arm with the fingers of the left hand in the "sword" position. Then, with these movements repeated, step again with the right leg, left leg, right leg, and left leg, with both arms spinning continuously.

二十三．白馬飛蹄

23 - **White horse flying hoof.**

After the final step of the left leg, once
more, swing your right arm in a large counter-
clockwise circular motion, then, shoot your
right sword fingers to the back, look over
your right shoulder, and sweep the right leg
upward. (The name of the movement should
indicate the power of the kick. Anyone ever
been kicked by a horse lately?)

24 - Spin the body, hooking hands, left stomping kick.

Put the right foot down, turn the body to the left, and momentarily shift into a left T-stance. Then after making a downward swinging hooking motion with the left hand, throw a left leg kick. Both hands are now in the crane's beak position. (The choice of doing a heel kick or a toe kick is up to the practitioner although the Chinese characters indicate a heel kick.)

二十五，双龍吐鬚

25 - Twin dragons spit their beards.

Put the left leg on the ground and shift into a left bow stance. Thrust both left and right sword fingers forward at shoulder level.

back view

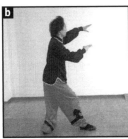

二十六，回头一指十字腿

26 - Turn the head, single finger, "Ten" character leg strike.

Turn the body to the right so that you now face in the opposite direction. As you momentarily set into a right T-stance, the left hand will make a sweeping motion from the left to the right, and the right sword fingers will draw back. Then pull back with the left hand, shoot out the sword fingers of the right hand, and kick out with a left leg toe kick.

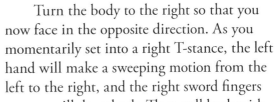

back view

二 十 七 ， 右 單 边 腿

27A - Right single kick.

Put the left leg down A) Move the right hand back in a counter-clockwise circle. Slap the right thigh with the back of the right hand, and then slap the instep of the right foot with the right palm. This is a right leg toe kick.

二十七，左單边腿

27B - Left single kick.

Put the right foot down. Move the left hand back in a clockwise circle. Slap the left thigh with the back of the left hand, and then slap the instep of the left foot with the left palm. Put the left foot on the ground.

二 十 八 . 二 起 腿

28 - Double kick.

Take a big step forward with the right leg, and then, pushing off with the right leg, swing the left leg up, followed by the right leg. While you are in the air, slap the right instep with the right palm. This is known as the "double kick." Land on the left leg.

56

二十九. 後盤腿

29 - Rear Coiling Leg (Back Twisted Kick).

Push off with the left leg, and while turning the body to the left, slap the inside of the left ankle with the palm of the right hand. The left arm will rise up naturally. Land on the right leg. (Although we translated the Chinese characters as "rear coiling leg," this could also have been called, 'rear twisted kick," or "back hook kick."

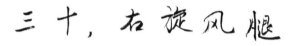

三十，右旋风腿

30 - Right tornado (whirlwind) kick.

While pushing off with the right leg, swing the left arm down in a large clockwise circle to create the momentum necessary to swing the left leg up in a counter-clockwise motion. The right leg follows the left leg and the right leg swings up in a counter-clockwise motion. While in the air, slap the left palm against the left side of the instep of the right foot.

三 十 一 . 撲 打 擒 虎 勢

31 - Protecting strike. Seize the tiger posture.

After doing the right leg tornado kick, drop down into a right scattered stance, and chop down with the edges of both palms simultaneously. (The name of this movement would indicate the great control that you should have over your opponent should you seize or chop him.)

back view

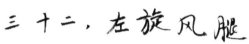

三十二，左旋风腿

32 - Left tornado kick.

Rise up and swing both arms using a counter-clockwise motion. Push off with the left leg, swing the right leg up, and follow with a left leg tornado kick. Slap the inside area of the left foot with the right palm.

back view

三十三. 撲打擒虎勢

33 - Protecting strike. Seize the tiger posture.

After doing the left leg tornado kick, drop down into a left scattered stance, and chop down with the edges of both palms simultaneously.

三十四．摟手單邊掌

34 - Scooping (left) hand. Single-edged (right) palm.

While rising up into a left bow stance, hook down and outward to your left with the left hand, and strike/push forward with the outer edge of the right hand.

三 十 五、海底 撈 月

35 - Pluck the moon from the bottom of the ocean.

Put your left hand in the guard position. While turning your body to the right so that you face in the opposite direction, make a counter-clockwise motion with the open right hand. Scoop down with your right hand with the palm facing upward while shifting into a right bow stance momentarily.

back view

back view

三十六、十字奔足

36 - "Ten" character charging (right) foot.

Turn to your left and shift back into a left bow stance momentarily. Move the left hand in a figure "8" motion by first bringing it down with the back of the hand facing the floor, and then up to slap the instep of the right foot. The right hand is open and held palm up and positioned at the side of the body.

back view

三十七，後盤腿

37 - Rear coiling leg.

Without putting the right foot down, push off with the left leg and slap the left heel area with the right palm. The left arm will rise up naturally. You will land on your right leg. (This is an optional move. Some practitioners prefer to delete this movement and go from #36 directly to #38. Either way is acceptable. Some practitioners prefer the forward momentum gained from going directly from #36 to #38, while others may prefer to develop their leg dexterity by adding in movement #37.

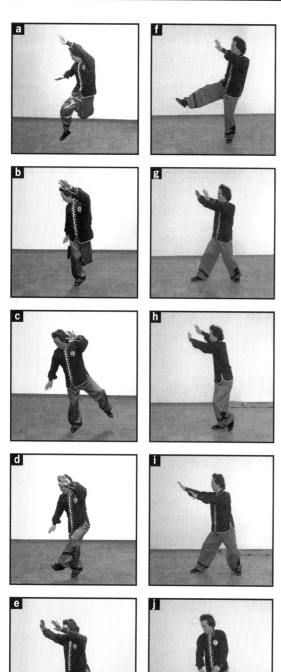

三十八．擺蓮腿

38 - Swinging lotus kick.

After the "rear coiling leg" kick, step down and forward with the left leg. Then step forward with the right leg. When the right foot steps down on the ground, push hard off the ground with the right leg so that you perform a jumping right leg lotus kick. Move your hands in a big clockwise circle (which may be for either blocking purposes and for the purpose of gathering momentum for the kick), and as the right leg kicks out in a clockwise motion, slap the instep of the right foot with the left and right palms quickly in succession.

38 - Continued

Alternatively, a practitioner may wish to omit the left step and right step and go immediately into the jumping right leg lotus kick by pushing off with the right leg after having landed on the right leg after completing the "rear coiling leg" kick of movement #37. Either way is acceptable. (When martial artists use the words "lotus kick," the implication is that the kick is one which moves from the inside to the outside, or an outward kick. A right leg lotus kick is one in which the right leg moves clockwise, and a left leg lotus kick is one in which the left leg moves counter-clockwise.)

三十九. 獅子大張咀

39 - Lion opens its mouth wide (Lion Yawning).

Land on the ground with the left leg coming down first, followed by the right leg. While shifting into a right bow stance, block up with an open right hand, and strike with the outer edge of the left hand.

68

back view

四十，四身掛打

40A -Turn the body, hanging strike (right palm).

Turn to your right, put the left hand in the guard position, and moving the right arm in a clockwise motion, strike down with the back of the right hand. Sit in a right bow stance. Notice that the name is different from movement 16A, but the actual move is the same.

back view

四十 , 鈎竿勢

40B - Hooking pole posture (right hook).

This is the same movement as in #16B. Withdraw the right hand slightly in a counter-clockwise motion, and then raise it up to strike with the back of the wrist. The right hand will become a crane's beak as you sit into a horse stance. The left hand remains in the guard position

四十一. 撲打擒虎勢

41 - Protecting strike. Seize the tiger posture.

Stamp the right foot and advance the left leg forward so that you sit in a left scattered stance. While moving ahead, chop forward and down with both palms simultaneously.

四十二 · 摟手單邊掌

42 - Scooping (left) hand Single-edged (right) palm.

While rising up into a left bow stance, the left hand clears the way by reaching forward and then hooking down and to your left side. The right hand strikes straight ahead with the outer edge of the right hand.

back view

四十三．右擺蓮腿

43A - Right swinging lotus kick.

Swing the right leg forward in a clockwise circle. Slap the instep of the right foot with the left palm and right palm quickly in succession.

73

四十三．左擺蓮腿

43B -Left swinging lotus kick.

Place the right foot down, swing the left leg forward in a counter-clockwise circle and slap the instep of the left foot with the right palm and left palm quickly in succession.

side view

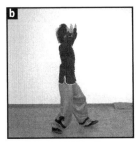

四十四，马到功成双钩势

44 - Horse arrives victoriously (Horse arrives with success) Double hooking posture.

Place the left foot down. Bring the arms together (right over left) and hook downward with both hands while kicking forward and upward with the right heel. Keep some of your weight back as you must prepare yourself for the next move which goes in the opposite direction.

四十五．單手右擺蓮

45 - Single hand, right sweeping lotus (hand).

Bring the right leg back and turn your body to your right. Swing the right arm, followed by the left arm, in a downward arc, to be followed by an upward arc as the motion is continued. Dip the body down and put your weight on your right leg so that you gather momentum for the next move. (Although this movement is mentioned in the Chinese characters as its own movement, some would find movement #45 as merely preparation for movement #46, and would not consider it a separate movement, so closely are movements #45 and #46 linked.)

四十六．燕子穿簾

46 - Swallow flies through the curtain.

Then, push off strongly with the right leg. The left leg will swing forward, followed quickly by the swing of the back of the right leg as you spin yourself completely in the air. Martial artists commonly call this the "butterfly" kick.

四十七．双风贯耳

47 - Double wind strikes the ears.

Land on the left leg and shift into a right bow stance. Swing both arms backward and then forward in a circular arc to strike the opponent's temples with the knuckles of both your hands.

side view

四 十 八 . 金 鸡 拍 翅

48 - Golden rooster flaps its wings.

Lift the left leg and do a front heel kick. Immediately after the kick passes chest level, clap both hands together under the kicking leg.

四十九. 一字腿

49 - "One" character leg.

Bring the left leg back and drop into the leg position commonly known as the "split." Place the open left hand behind your back and push the right palm into the air as shown.

back view

五十 · 磨盤腿

50 - Grinding, coiling leg.

Quickly, hop the left leg forward so that the weight is momentarily on the left leg. You may do this with or without the aid of your hands. You are now in a right scattered stance, your left hand is on your left side and your right hand is on your right side.

Swing the right leg in a counter-clockwise motion so that the right leg passes in front of the left leg and then under the left leg as the left foot is raised up momentarily, so that the right leg may revolve in a complete circle. You have now returned to a right scattered stance and both your hands are now in front of you.

五十一．鐵牛耕地

51 - Iron ox plows the earth.

Shift your body so that your weight is now over your right leg. You are now in a left scattered stance. As you change stance, the right hand reaches down and becomes open (palm up), while the left hand is open (palm down). Pull the right back and shoot the left hand down as both hands clench into fists. The right hand is pulling, while the left hand is striking. (As an ox is strong, so too should you perform this movement with the same strength and determination.)

五十二、舞花右穿心腿

52 - Right (hand) dancing with the flowers. Penetrating heart kick (right leg).

From your low stance, rise up and reach forward with both hands (palms down). Both hands move together in a clockwise circle. When pulling back, the right palm will turn face up and the left palm will stay face down while both hands clench into fists in a grasping, twisting motion. While pulling back in with the hands, kick out and upward with the right heel.

83

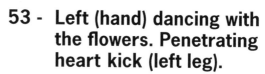

五十三. 舞花左穿心腿

53 - Left (hand) dancing with the flowers. Penetrating heart kick (left leg).

Place the right foot on the ground. Reach forward with both hands (palms down) and move the hands together in a counterclockwise circle. When pulling back, the left palm will turn face up and the right palm will stay face down while both hands clench into fists in a grasping, twisting motion. While pulling back in with the hands, kick out and upward with the left heel.

84

五十四．飛腿落地双炮捶

54A - Flying leg, fall to the ground.

Bring the left leg back, and using the right leg as a base from which to push off, swing the left leg up, and follow it with a right jumping heel kick. As the left leg swings up, cross both arms in an "X" fashion, right forearm below the left forearm, and swing both arms up and outward. The right leg kicks out with the heel while you are in the air.

五十四．飛腿落地双炮捶

54B - Double uplifting hammers (uppercut).

Both arms then deliver uppercut punches as you fall forward into a right bow stance.

五十五. 右偷步獅子抱球

55A - Right leg stealing a step, lion holds the ball

Turning your body slightly to your right, step the right leg behind the left leg so that you sit into a left T-stance at a 45-degree angle. As if holding a ball, turn both hands in a clockwise circle so that the left palm ends in a face down position at chest level, and the right palm ends in a face up position at stomach level.

五十五. 左偷步獅子抱球

55B - Left leg stealing a step, lion holds the ball.

The next move is the matching move on the opposite side. Now, turning your body slightly to your left, step the left leg behind the right leg so that you sit into a right T-stance at a 45-degree angle. As if holding a ball, turn both hands in a counter-clockwise circle so that the right palm ends in a face down position at chest level, and the left palm ends in a face up position at stomach level.

五十六、左右舞花倒退步

56 - Left and right hands dancing with the flowers. Retreating step.

While stepping back with the right foot into a left cat stance, turn both hands using a clockwise motion. The left hand will end up hooking downward from the front and then swinging to your left side, while the right hand will end up pushing up from the inside and then out to your right side.

side view

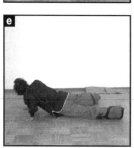

五十七. 撲地側身劃腿

57 - Crash to the ground. Slanted (sideways) body. Scraping legs.

Push off with the left leg and throw your right leg forward, followed by the left leg. While turning your body to your left, both of your legs will slide forward. Your weight will be supported by your hands (similar to the "push-up" position), and the balls of your feet. Turn your head slightly to your right and look over your right shoulder.

back view

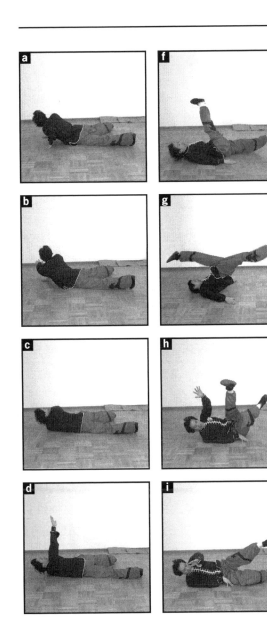

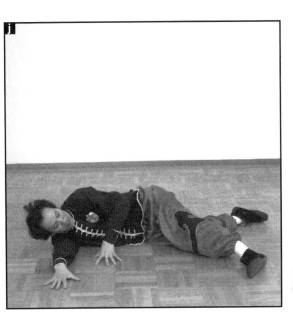

五 十 八 . 左 金 較 剪

58A - Left golden scissors movement (kick).

Reach your left hand past and over the right hand and momentarily lie on your left side. Then reach the right hand to your right side (while rolling on your back), and spin your legs in a clockwise circular motion, right leg followed by the left leg. This is called a "leg flower" or "leg scissors" technique. You will complete the motion with the body lying on its right side, the left hand moving alongside the right hand, and the left leg over the right leg.

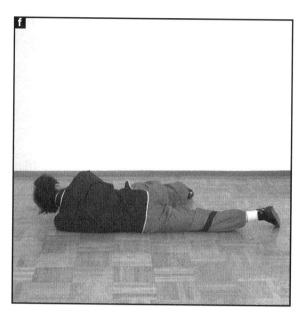

五十八. 右金較剪

58B - Right golden scissors movement (kick).

Now reach the left hand to your left side (while rolling on your back), spin your legs in a counter-clockwise circular motion, left leg followed by the right leg. You will complete the motion with the body lying on its left side, the right hand moving alongside the left hand, and the right leg over the left leg.

五 十 八 . 左 金 鉸 剪

58C - Left golden scissors movement (kick).

Now reach the right hand back to your right side (while rolling on your back), and spin your legs in a clockwise circular motion, right leg followed by the left leg. You will complete the motion with the body lying on its right side, the left hand moving alongside the right hand, and the left leg over the right leg.

五十九．起身

59A - Raise the body.

Use both hands to push against the floor to raise your body. As the body is rising up, hop the right foot in towards your chest, so that you are in a left scattered stance. Your weight is on the right heel, and both hands are braced against the floor.

五十九. 右单边腿

59B - Right single leg (kick).

Rise up and make a counter-clockwise clearing motion with the left hand. Then, slap the instep of the right foot with your right palm.

五十九. 左单边腿

59C - Left single leg (kick).

Put the right foot down. Now, slap the instep of the left foot with the left palm.

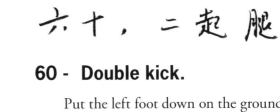

六十， 二起腿

60 - Double kick.

Put the left foot down on the ground. Take a big step forward with the right leg, and then, pushing off with the right leg, swing the left leg up, followed by the right leg. You are in the air. Slap the right instep with the right palm. Land on the left leg.

六 十 一、 後 盤 腿

61 - Rear coiling leg.

Push off with the left leg, and while turning the body to the left, slap the inside of the left ankle with the palm of the right hand. The left arm will rise up naturally. Land on the right leg.

六 十 二. 旋 风 腿

62 - Right tornado kick.

While pushing off with the right leg, swing the left arm down in a large clockwise circle to create the momentum necessary to swing the left leg up in a counter-clockwise motion. The right leg follows the left leg and the right leg swings up in a counter-clockwise motion. While in the air, slap the left palm against the left side of the instep of the right foot.

六 十 三 . 左 擺 蓮 腿

63A -Left swinging lotus leg.

Step down with the right leg. Bring up the left leg in a large, swinging counter-clockwise motion and do a left lotus kick. Slap both of your palms, right first then left, against the outside of the left foot.

六十三. 右擺蓮腿

63B -Right swinging lotus leg.

Step down with the left leg. Bring up the right leg in a large, swinging clockwise motion and do a right lotus kick. Slap both of your palms, left first then right, against the outside of your right foot.

六十四、回身左掛面腿

64A -Turn the body. Left leg striking the face.

Turn your body to your right and face the opposite direction. Put your right foot down. Your left leg will swing in a clockwise direction (left crescent kick) and your right palm will slap the instep of the left foot.

六十四、右掛面腿

64B -Right leg striking the face.

Put the left foot down. Your right leg will swing in a counter-clockwise direction (right crescent kick) and your left palm will slap the instep of the right foot.

六十五. 猴子鬧癢

65A -Monkey disturbed by itch (A).

As you put the right foot down on its heel, slap the right elbow with the palm of the left hand.

六十五. 猴子閙癢

65B -Monkey disturbed by itch (B).

Then, slap the back of the right hand into the left palm as you push off with the right leg.

六十五. 提麻蜂

65C - Catches the wasp.

As you are jumping into the air, slap the back of both hands against your thighs, rise up into the air and clap your hands together as you come down to the ground.

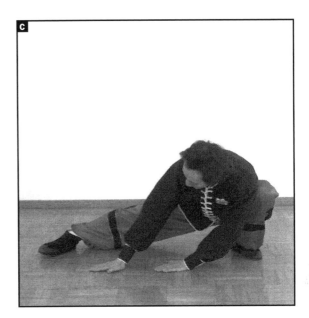

六十六. 拍地飛沙

66 - Strike the ground. Flying sand.

Slap the ground with both palms as you land in a right scattered stance.

六十七. 旋风腿

67 - Right tornado kick.

Rise up quickly and putting the weight on the right leg, swing the left leg in a counter-clockwise circle. Push off with the right leg, swing the right leg in a large counter-clockwise circle and slap the instep of the right foot with the left palm.

六 十 八 . 鉄 牛 耕 地

68 - Iron ox plows the earth.

As you land on the left leg and shift the weight to your right leg, drop down into a left scattered stance. As you shift into the left scattered stance, pull back with the right hand and punch down with the left.

六十九. 舞花英雄獨立

69 - Dancing with the flowers. Hero stands on one leg.

Rise up. As you shift into a left bow stance, make a downward clearing motion with the left fist, and swing your right arm from the right side to the left side. This movement is sometimes known as "striking the tiger." Then, while stamping the right foot on the ground, swing the right fist downward and raise up the left knee. The left foot may be turned in a slight hooking position if the practitioner so desires.

六十九. 舞花英雄獨立

69 - Dancing with the flowers. Hero stands on one leg. (continued)

To complete this movement, continue to swing the right arm in a counter-clockwise motion until the right fist is above the head, and finally place the left fist in a clockwise downward arc to the outside of the left knee. Blocking with the left and striking with the right hand above your head is also known as "Striking the tiger."

七十． 退步穿掌

70A -Step back. Piercing palm.

As you step back with the left leg at a 45-degree angle, drop the hand forward in an open palm position. Then, shoot the left hand forward (palm thrust) so that the back of the left hand touches the right palm. The fingertips of the left hand may be extended slightly beyond the outer boundary of the right hand.

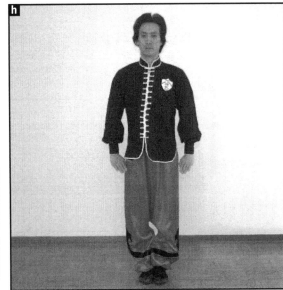

七十．收式

70B -Closing posture.

Withdraw the right leg to the side of the left leg; slap the outside of both hands against the thighs as you bend your knees. Stand up, raise both hands above the head, and then push down with both palms. Bow, then stand at attention, and the set is completed.

Shaolin #1: Selected Applications

Shaolin #1: Selected Applications

Note that the applications shown are basic level applications and that your own personal instructor may show you applications of a more advanced nature. Remember that a book can never replace an experienced instructor who is working one-on-one with you. Quick reaction time, a good tactile sense and your choice of the right opportunity to launch your technique should result in a successfully applied technique.

1 - Revolving hands dancing with the flowers. Sitting tiger posture.

Hook the opponent's left hand with your left hand and use a right palm strike against his unprotected left side.

2 - Phoenix circling the nest.

If the opponent steps in aggressively to attack with a right palm strike, you can simply sidestep to avoid the attack.

3 - Immortal man pays respect with a salute.

If the opponent grabs your neck and shoulder area tightly, raise both your hands and brush downward with both arms to break his grip on you. Then, you may strike his head with your hands. Although the movement in the set utilizes a right fist strike, you may also clap his head with both your hands, or even strike with both fists.

3 -   Continued.

4 - Hands dancing with the flowers. Single hooking hand (right).

Use your left hand to block or grab his left hand, and strike the left side of his head with the back of your hand.

As the movement in this set is of a continuous swinging motion, you could also immobilize his right hand and strike the right side of his head with the back of your hand.

If he strikes with his right hand, grab or parry it with your left hand, and use a crane's beak strike to his forehead.

5 - Sitting horse listens to the wind.

Block his right hand with your right hand, step forward with your left leg and chop at his throat with the blade edge of the left hand . This is an illustration of a very common method in martial art, which is to use your attacking hand to slide up the opponent's arm to strike at your target.

Continued next page

6 - Covering the heart, elbow strike. (Elbow strike to the heart).

Suppose the opponent grabs your left wrist with his left hand. You may pull your arm back, thus causing his left arm to straighten. Then, use your right elbow to push up against the back of his left elbow, to cause discomfort to his left arm.

6 - continued

Another application of the same movement would be the following. If the opponent strikes you with his left hand, you could parry it with your own left hand, and strike him in the back with your right elbow.

Alternatively, you could block with your left hand and strike his head with your right elbow.

If the opponent is much taller than you are, you may have to leap up to strike the opponent in the head. As is typical in all martial arts, each technique needs to be modified to fit a particular situation or opponent.

7 - Pulling hook (hand), hanging strike (leg), pressing horse posture.

Parry his left hand strike with your left hand, use your right leg against the back of his left leg to unbalance him, and strike his throat with the fingertips of your right hand's crane's beak.

8 - Sitting horse listens to the wind. (Sit in horse, right palm strike).

Pull his left hand with your left hand, and chop him with the edge of your right hand.

9 - Steal a step. Connected links (palms). Penetrating arm (left palm).

Block his strike downward with your right palm, and strike out with the edge of your left palm

c

10 - Right crashing palm. Left heel kick.

Sometimes, movements in martial art forms may be used against multiple opponents. In this case, use the right palm strike against the throat of one opponent, and use the side kick against the other opponent. In this case, the side kick is directed to the chest.

The height of your strikes may depend on where you feel your opponent is most vulnerable. In this case, the side kick is directed to the throat .

11 - Swinging kick to the face.

Some of the techniques such as this one are self-explanatory. As the opponent steps in, jump up and use the right leg tornado kick to strike the opponent in the face.

15 - Black tiger crashes through the mountain.

Block upward with your right arm and step forward to strike him with your left fist.

16A - Sparrow hawk turns its body.

As the opponent steps in to strike you, turn your body to the right, thus taking away his intended target, and strike him on his head with the back of your right hand.

16B - Hooking pole posture.

If the opponent attempts to block your previous strike, withdraw your right hand, and use the back of the crane's beak to strike him under his chin.

19 - Mount Tai crashes down!

Use your left hand to block his left-handed strike. Your left hand should utilize a counter-clockwise twisting motion. As your left hand turns his arm, strike down hard with the back of the right fist.

20 - Turn the body, hooking hands, left heel kick.

Hook his right hand strike with your left hand, and use a left leg side kick against his unprotected flank.

23 - White horse flying hoof.

This movement follows directly from movement #22. You block his strike with your right hand, and kick to his lower region with your right leg.

Alternatively, you may block his strike with your right hand, and then use the flat part of the right foot to strike him high.

... Or you may use the heel of the right foot to strike him even higher.

26 - Turn the head, single finger, "Ten" character leg strike.

If the opponent strikes you with his right arm, parry it down or to the side with your left hand, kick him in the lower region with the left instep, and thrust the fingertips of your right hand towards his eyes.

32 - Left tornado kick.

Jump up and do a circular kick to his head with your left leg.

33 - Protecting strike.
Seize the tiger posture.

This move follows directly from movement #32. After falling down from the left tornado kick, you may either chop down with both arms ….

… or grab his right arm with your right hand, and then chop him with your left hand.

34 - Scooping (left) hand. Single-edged (right) palm.

Hook his left hand away and to the side with your left hand, and use the edge of the right palm to strike him in the face.

35 - Pluck the moon from the bottom of the ocean.

If your opponent attacks you from above, reach down and counter his move by grabbing his groin from below.

38 - Swinging lotus kick.

Jump forward and use your right leg to strike him high. Although kicks like this are very powerful, they must be properly set up in order for them to be effective.

39 - Lion opens its mouth wide. (Lion yawning).

As the opponent attempts to either strike you or grab you with his right arm, block up with your right arm and strike to his face with your left hand.

43A - Right swinging lotus kick.

Parry his right hand strike or grab with your right arm, and use your right leg to attack his unprotected flank.

45-46 - Single hand, right sweeping lotus (hand). Swallow flies through the curtain.

This is a surprise technique and a powerful move. Use your right hand to clear the area or to distract your opponent. As you spin your body in the air, use the back of your right leg to strike the opponent.

This move should be done sparingly and only if you have practiced it many, many times. If you are not careful, what will happen is that your opponent will simply step back and attack you when you land. Be careful!

48 - Golden rooster flaps its wings.

As the opponent reaches out to grab you, you can grab his hands, pull him in, and kick out at his chest or head with your left heel.

51 - Iron ox plows the earth.

As the opponent attempts to kick you, grab his leg, pull him and strike his thigh with your left fist.

Alternatively, you may punch him in a more vulnerable spot.

52 - Right (hand) dancing with the flowers. Penetrating heart kick (right leg).

Block his right arm by grabbing his wrist with your right hand, and pressing down on his elbow with your left hand, pull him in slightly and kick out with your right heel.

55A -Right leg stealing a step, lion holds the ball.

Grab his right wrist with your right hand, and then twist his right wrist with your right hand as you press down on his elbow with your left hand.

55B -Left leg stealing a step, lion holds the ball.

As is typical in many martial art forms, movements are done on both sides so as to promote health, and also so that you will be able to apply the technique from either your left or right side.

Grab his left wrist with your left hand, and then twist his left wrist with your left hand as you press down on his elbow with your right hand.

57 - Crash to the ground. Slanted (sideways) body. Scraping legs.

Push off with your legs and throw your body forward. You may either attack him by using your feet to strike his knee or shin, or you may attempt to hook his legs in preparation for the next movement.

58A -Left golden scissors movement (kick).

After you hook his legs, you may press the back of your right leg against the front of his left knee, thus causing him to fall.

58A -Left golden scissors movement (kick).

Alternatively, you could press the back of your right leg against the back of his right knee, thus causing him also to buckle and fall.

Continued next page

65 - Monkey disturbed by itch. Catches the wasp.

If the opponent attempts to grab you, strike upwards with your right elbow and hit his chin.

Then strike down with the back of the right hand to hit his face.

As a finishing move, jump up and clap both of his ears with the palms of your hands.

Alternatively, you could simply clap his ears with both hands without jumping.

69 - Dancing with the flowers. Hero stands on one leg.

Grab his right arm with your left hand, and drive upwards with your left knee into his lower region. Done properly and with force, this move should render his attack completely impotent.

Use your right fist to strike his head.

Names of Movements of Shaolin #1 in Chinese Calligraphy

by Paul Eng

一. 滚手舞花坐虎势

二. 凤凰旋窝

三. 仙人拱手

四. 舞花单钩手

五. 坐马听风

六. 护心肘

七. 挑钩掛打披马势

八. 坐马听风

九. 偷步连环通臂掌

十. 右撑掌左蹬腿

十一. 掛面腿

十二. 拍地飞沙

十三. 磨盘腿

十四. 扑腿小闯门

十五. 黑虎闯山

十六、鹞子翻身

十七、挑钩掛打披马势

十八、左蹬足

十九、泰山压顶

二十、回身钩手左蹬足

二十一、挑钩掛打披马势

二十二、乌龙摆尾倒退步

二十三、白马飞蹄

二十四、转身钩手左蹬腿

二十五、双龙吐须

二十六，回头一指十字腿

二十七、右单边腿

二十七、左单边腿

二十八、二起腿

二十九、后盘腿

166

三十．右旋风腿

三十一．撲打擒虎勢

三十二．左旋风腿

三十三．撲打擒虎勢

三十四．攢手单边掌

三十五．海底撈月

三十六．十字奔足

三十七．後盤腿

三十八．擺蓮腿

三十九．獅子大張咀

四十．回身掛打鈎竿勢

四十一．撲打擒虎勢

四十二．攢手单边掌

四十三．右擺蓮腿

四十三．右擺蓮腿

四十四．马到功成双钩势

四十五．单手右摆莲

四十六．燕子穿簾

四十七．双风贯耳

四十八．金鸡拍翅

四十九．一字腿

五十．磨盘腿

五十一．铁牛耕地

五十二．舞花右穿心腿

五十四．飞腿落地双炮捶

五十三．舞花左穿心腿

五十五．右偷步狮子抱球

五十五．左偷步狮子抱球

五十六．左右舞花倒退步

五十七．扑地侧身劈腿

六十七．旋风腿
六十八．铁牛耕地
六十九．舞花英雄獨立
七十．　退步穿掌
七十．　收式

Sweeps in the Northern Shaolin Style

Sweeps in the Northern Shaolin Style

The Northern Shaolin Style is replete with leg sweeping techniques. The sweep may be used as a subtle set-up technique to unbalance your opponent, or it may also be used to make him fall to the ground by taking his legs out from under him. The possibilities are endless.

Typically, northern styles have a much higher number of sweeps than southern styles, and I would like to present some numeric information on these movements. I present this knowing full well it may be of scant interest to a general reader, however it may interest some. In the small chance that an aficionado of the Northern Shaolin Style has ever wondered about this type of thing, here is the information.

I will characterize the sweeps as left leg (L) or right leg (R), and as a forward sweep (F) or backward sweep (B). I also did not want to break the sweeps down in terms of sweeps from a standing position as opposed to a squatting position, etc.

The raw data from which the tables will be constructed is given below. Each number listed after the name of the form will measure how much area is swept out by the leg. For a half sweep I shall write "½," for a three-quarter sweep I shall write "¾," and for a full sweep I shall write "1". Below each number I will write either L or R or F or B depending on what type of sweep it is. The total listed at the side will indicate how much area is swept out for each form.

Short Forms

Shaolin #6   ½ + ¾ + ½ = 1¾
                 R   L   R
                 F   B   B

Shaolin #5   ½ = ½
                 L
                 B

Shaolin #7   ½ + 1 = 1½
                 R   L
                 F   B

Shaolin #4   ½ + 1 = 1½
                 R   L
                 F   B

Shaolin #8   1 + ½ + 1 = 2½
                 R   L   L
                 B   B   B

Long Forms

Shaolin #3 ½ + ½ + 1 + ½ + ½ = 3
R R L L R
B F B B B

Shaolin #2 1 + 1 + ½ + 1 + ½ + 1 = 5
L R R L L R
B F F B F B

Shaolin #1 1 + 1 = 2
R R
F F

Shaolin #9 ½ + ¾ + 1 = 2¼
R R L
B F B

Shaolin #10 ½ + ½ + ½ + ½ + ½ + ½ = 3
L R R L R L
B B B B B F

We can see that the set that sweeps out the most area of the shorter forms would be Shaolin #8, and the set that sweeps out the most area of the longer forms would be Shaolin #2

And for the numerically inclined, for the five short forms the average number of revolutions swept out is 1.55, and for the five long forms the average number is 3.05. Taking all ten sets together, the average number of revolutions is 2.3 with a standard deviation of 1.15.

If we simply looked at the number of sweeps, we would have the following information.

Shaolin #6:   3 sweeps
Shaolin #7:   2 sweeps
Shaolin #8:   3 sweeps
Shaolin #5:   1 sweeps
Shaolin #4:   2 sweeps

Shaolin #3:   5 sweeps
Shaolin #2:   6 sweeps
Shaolin #1:   2 sweeps
Shaolin #9:   3 sweeps
Shaolin #10:   6 sweeps

So the average number of sweeps in the short forms would be 2.2 with a standard deviation of 0.7483, and the average number of sweeps in the long forms would be 4.4 with a standard deviation of 1.6248. Overall, the average number of sweeps would be 3.3 with a standard deviation 1.6763. This would make sense as the longer forms are approximately twice the length of the shorter forms.

By and large, in the beginning five short Shaolin forms, the most common sweep combination is the right leg front sweep followed by the left leg back sweep, and this combination is seen in Shaolin #6, Shaolin #7, Shaolin #4, Shaolin #3 and Shaolin #2. As a short note on sweeps in the style, I would like to show the following sets of small tables from which we can create further tables to summarize the information even more.

Short Forms

Shaolin #6

	Left	Right
Front	0	1
Back	1	1

Shaolin #7

	Left	Right
Front	0	1
Back	1	0

Shaolin #8

	Left	Right
Front	0	0
Back	2	1

Shaolin #5

	Left	Right
Front	0	0
Back	1	0

Shaolin #4

	Left	Right
Front	0	1
Back	1	0

Long Forms

Shaolin #3

	Left	Right
Front	0	1
Back	2	2

Shaolin #2

	Left	Right
Front	1	2
Back	2	1

Shaolin #1

	Left	Right
Front	0	2
Back	0	0

Shaolin #9

	Left	Right
Front	0	1
Back	1	1

Shaolin #10

	Left	Right
Front	1	0
Back	2	3

The forms Shaolin #2 and Shaolin #9 both have a right leg "grind the bowl" sweep in them, while as mentioned before, Shaolin #1 has two of them. Shaolin #3, Shaolin #2 and Shaolin #10 have the greatest amounts of sweeps in total, with 5, 6, and 6 respectively, that is, if we are simply totaling up the number of sweeps.

If we count up the number of revolutions covered in the sweeps, with say, a half sweep counting as 1/2, a three-quarters sweep as 3/4, and a full sweep as 1, we have the following information.

	Left	Right
Front	½ + ½ = 1	½ + ½ + ... + ¾ = 6.25
Back	¾ + 1 + ... + ½ = 10.5	½ + 1 + ... + ½ = 5.50

This should make it apparent as to why many who practice the style will become more proficient with the right leg forward sweep and the left leg back sweep.

Similarly, if we simply totaled up the number of sweeps, we would have the following tables.

Short Forms

	Left	Right
Front	0	3
Back	6	2

Long Forms

	Left	Right
Front	2	6
Back	7	7

All Forms Combined

	Left	Right
Front	2	9
Back	13	9

For those who know the entire system, the right leg full back sweep from an upright horse stance in Shaolin #8 is a movement that may prove relatively more difficult as it does not occur very often in the style and the practitioner does not get to practice it as much. For those who practice this style, this movement may need to be practiced on its own if we want to have the same facility with this sweep as we do with the others. If a practitioner wants the facility of doing sweeps with either leg well, he must practice some of these techniques outside the confines of the forms for his own benefit.

Notice also that there are more back sweeps than front sweeps. To be specific, there are 11 front sweeps and 22 back sweeps. If we were to total up the sweeps according to which leg they were done with, we can see that 18 sweeps are executed with the right leg and 15 sweeps are done with the left leg. Lastly, remember that there are many variations and different lineages in the Northern Shaolin Style, so keep in mind that these numbers may not exactly match the movements in your own forms.

Acknowledgements

Acknowledgements

Doing this book has been a pleasure; in retrospect it's more of a pleasure after the task is finished than during, because some things involved in creating and making this book were just plain hard work! And I'm sure all of the people who helped me feel the same way! It has been a learning experience for me and I would like to take the time to thank the people who graciously gave of their time. My time was … uh,… free.

First, I'd like to thank Michelle Dwyer, a seasoned instructor and lifelong martial arts professional. She has graced this book with a fine essay on Northern Shaolin. I have known Michelle for many years and would like to thank her for her years of selfless friendship. I look forward to many more.

If I mention Michelle I must also mention her partner, Bruce Hopkins. Without the computer expert, there just ain't no book! Thanks for your many hours of help. We've got another graphic artist here and this one isn't temperamental! How can that be?

Master Paul Eng applied his martial expertise to help fine tune the translation of the names. His knowledge, experience, and depth of understanding of the martial arts are extraordinary. As usual, he also applied his calligraphy skills which are apparent throughout the book. I checked the calligraphy in detail by… well, by asking Master Eng to check the calligraphy again. His breadth of knowledge is amazing, and you, the reader, have indeed benefited! It's always a pleasure to visit with Master Paul Eng. By the way, we went fist to fist (once), and it shouldn't surprise anyone that … he bruised my knuckles. I felt like asking for one of those little stickers that say "I didn't cry." I'd also like to mention that while Master Eng was serving our country in a foreign land in the 1960's, I was either busy playing in a sandbox in Huntington Park on Nob Hill or watching black and white television, full-time. Three guesses as to who the real martial arts man is, and hint, it ain't me. A big salute to Master Paul Eng.

For the photos in the applications part of the book, I'd like to thank Tom "Pilot" Busby, Scott Jensen, "Big" Steve Ryan, and Michael Shaman. These are all of my teacher's students and they were very gracious in allowing me to demonstrate the applications on them. I know I couldn't ever really apply these techniques on them, but I appealed to their "inner actor." They also asked if they could pay less the next month. Guys, you're funny., and I really enjoy your cents of humor. Now back to work. Let's see who's who now. Tom is the guy with the mustache, Scott is the traditional kung fu man… Steve is the tall karate expert, now a kung fu expert … and Michael, the internal instructor, is the… other one. See if you can match them up now.

I'd also like to thank Sir John Sutherland for helping with the text. Although he is descended from the great highland clans of Scotland, in his magnanimity he has seen fit to help me with the English, trader that he is. With his assistance, this book will now not be seen as being written by someone like me who was barely able to get out of school. Thanks for the help, Sir John. I also notice that whenever Sir John says "The master is in rare form today," I'm usually not doing anything physically, but just making comments to fill the air. I quietly seethe but can do nothing, considering the daunting prowess of the man, both verbal and physical.

Phillip Wong took all the photos (again, and again, and again), and the proof is on the pages. He's done this so many times now, that he's since gone into mind reading, or at least reading my mind. I'll go, "It should look something like this," and he'll say, "Got it." I'll say, "Are you ready now?" and he'll reply, "I just did, take a look." Whoa! He's got this down big time, wouldn't you say? Thanks Phil.

It is also important for me to acknowledge Sifu Ken Hui, an important representative of the Northern Shaolin clan in southern California He is the teacher of Sifu Kisu.

I would also like to thank Grandmaster Chan Kwok Wai for his kind permission in allowing the use of the photos of Great Grandmaster Yim in the book "Shaolin #5, Martial Skill." One of his senior students, Mr. Roberto Baptista, kindly aided me in my communication with Master Chan. Master Chan is known as the "Father of Chinese Martial Art" in Brazil.

Made in the USA
San Bernardino, CA
30 November 2013